Made in the USA
Monee, IL
10 May 2021

68226434R10068